Sower on the Cliffs

Sower on the Cliffs

Poems and Drawings

Helen Mirkil

B&P

BookArts Press
2013

Printed in the United States of America
First Edition

Published by

B&P

BookArts Press
www.book-arts-press.com

The text of this book is composed in Cochin,
with the title set in Academy Engraved.
Cover drawing reproduced by Profiles Studio.
Book design by Veronica Miller & Associates.

ISBN 978-0-9795861-5-6

To Brisaph,

may I have this dance?

CONTENTS

"My food," said Jesus, "is to do the will of Him who sent me and to finish His work… open your eyes and look at the fields!"

"A sower went out to sow his seed: and as he sowed, some fell by the way side; and it was trodden down, and the fowls of the air devoured it. And some fell upon a rock; and as soon as it sprung up, it withered away, because it lacked moisture. And some fell upon thorns: and the thorns sprang up with it, and choked it. And others fell on good ground, and sprang up, and bare fruit an hundredfold."

"Those who sow in tears will reap with songs of joy."

(John 4: 34-38; Luke 8: 4-15; Psalm 126:5)

bread of heaven

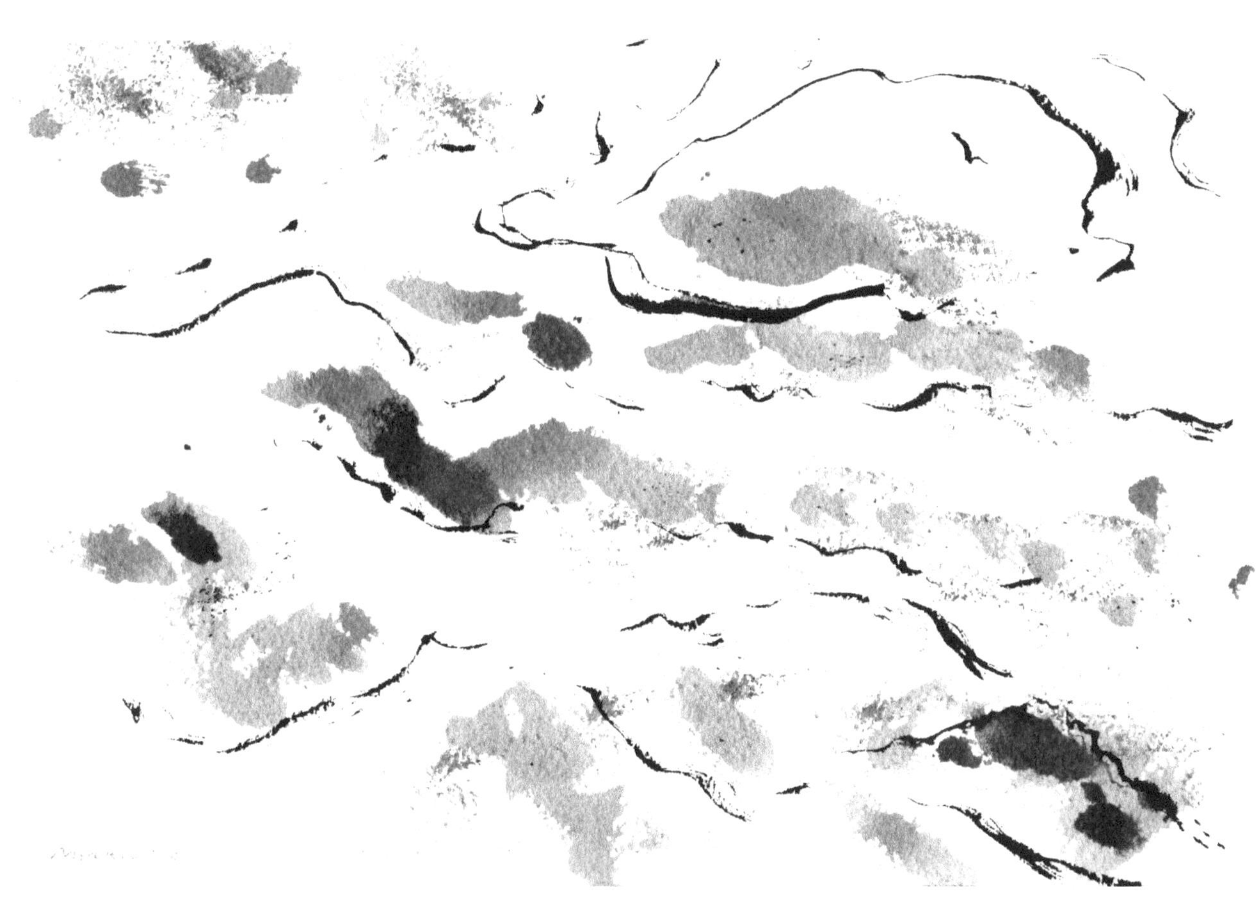

HE FEEDS HER
(for John Warren)

Every Friday
an Italian meal
learned at her apronside,
when he was half her size.
Now she's the smaller

ninety pounds
and eyes bright as a child's,
eager to taste of life,
hear a story told
by her Johnny boy.

On Fridays she waits,
imagines a wiry boy,
powder up to his elbows
helping Nonna flatten pasta
with her wooden rolling pin.

Ooooooeee!
How the hours fly by!
Again the aroma… my lasagna!
Thanks be to God
he's here again! My Johnny boy!

THE TUB
(for Vera)

Ease your toes in,
see the steam risin'!
Set yourself down, down home

let the waters sing low
to those world-weary bones,
lean over, lean down

dip your face
in the place, let your mind fly
home, to the age-old place

you're cells being formed
and there is weightlessness,
you're all arms and legs

curled in your mama's belly,
sweetly held by the waters
of her lovely universe.

Can you see, child see,
can you, do you?
How the Lord, how He's always

proudly loved you,
'fore you were in here swimmin'
or your mama always leavin'

way back then He loved you
dear one, how He loved you,
back when you didn't

even know you was you.

BREAD OF HEAVEN

I listen, hear You say
I AM the bread of life,
follow me, eat of me,
drink from the well
of my living water.

If I sit at Your feet, Jeshua,
will my eyes be bright and clear
like the dear ones
who have nothing
but a passion for You?

Whoever comes to me
I will never turn away.
Thank You Lord! As a baby
my own mother handed me off.
Hold me Jesus!

My wounds are deep
yet with You I empty my jaws
to the heavens, my rage!
I am here wailing
in Your loving arms.

You see into me,
all there is to see.
I am afraid.
Then Your eyes speak
You are my beloved.

In Your light
I am loved.
I can dance in this broken world,
be with Your children,
wash their weary feet.

Be with me Jesus,
fountain of life,
Morning Star, I kneel
to Thee, O Holy Spirit
eternal breath of God.

little miracles

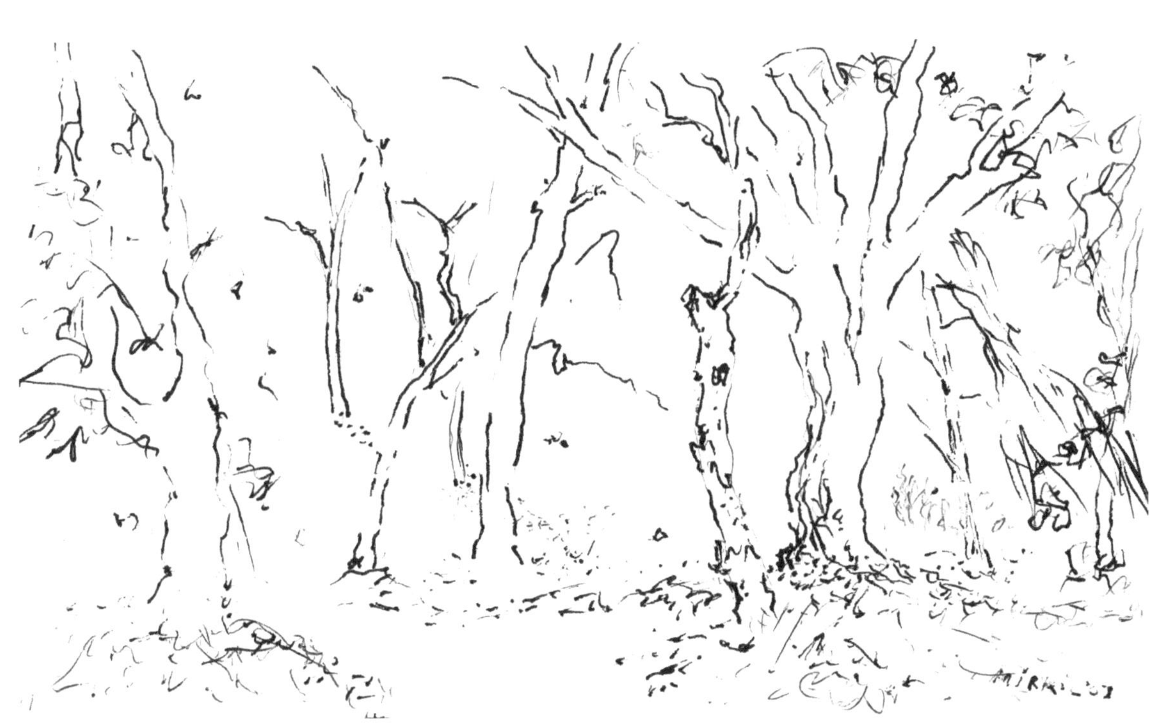

BE

The singing,
when twisted thoughts
flood the soul,
where is

the mountain,
where mist hovers,
bees hum, and wind
curls through junipers.

Be, friend,
in this peace,
in His sweetness

inside ancient lullabies.

ENFOLDING
(for Dee Dee)

Scarecrow arms
pulled out from under

abraded denim legs
tangled

with mud-tinted
ribbed feet

a jumbled lump
someone left behind

for slow, patient hands
to gather and immerse

scrub and spin
in a cylinder of warm

air and light,
the water-weary

limbs somersault,
twist, salsa, shimmy

do the funky monkey
with their insides out

and stunned,
for loving hands

will lift them
and enfold them,

make them new
and know them,

soothing, aged hands.

MY BROWN

The wild green and brown,
      the marsh, the fertile brown,
five tiny crabs
      raise one club-claw
to scuttle up the bank and down,
      absorb the richness of the brown

then scurry back to shade
      and spongy moss, a time to rest.
Cool shadows, breeze
      against my sun-blushed cheek,
chorus of the wild reeds
      where birds in evening

build their song
      in cover of the cedar trees.
When dusk rolls in
      at gentle end of gentle day
gray doves coo, fold their wings,
      bullfrog plucks his deepest strings

and crabs sleep safely, tucked away.
      Clouds of crimson signal me
for I'm only passing through —
      my slow reluctant steps retrace
the fertile green and brown,
      this lovely ground I've come to know.

Too soon, too soon
      the day-to-day will
dull my ears,
      drown my peace, my calm
yet I will carry brown
      and brown will shelter me

from heat of day
      and ever restless dreams of night,
so I'll sleep safely, tucked away.

soul mate

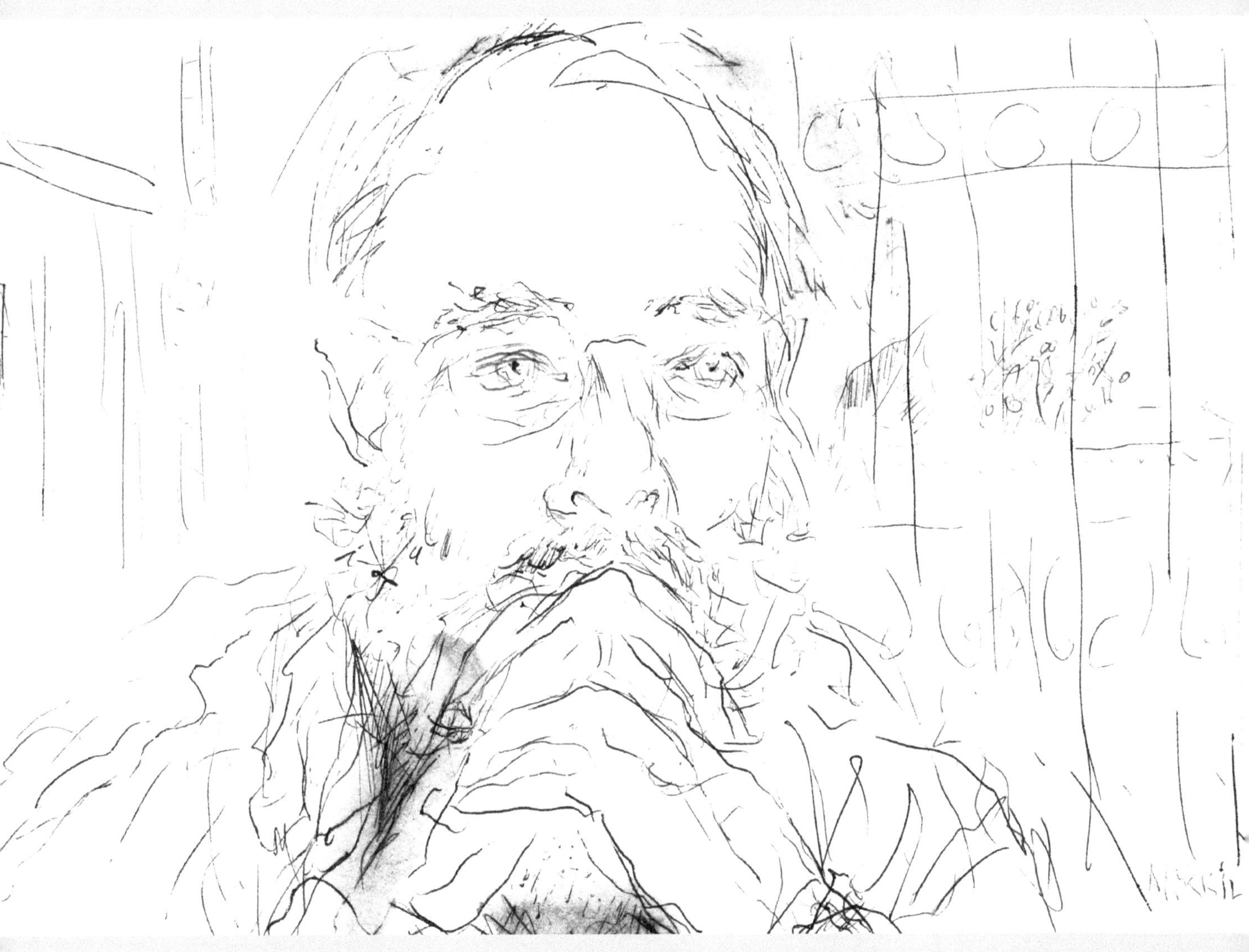

CAVE TALK

Those notes like words

you breathed into my ear —
those low-toned puffs of air

in dark and close, am I to hear

yet never really know?
There is a rift in Time

as four walls fade,

give way to rock face, painted horse
and buffalo.

No longer must a line divide

the earth from sky —
all questions melt away

as does the will.

Engaged, the sacred
waters flow —

ah, Ancient Heart!

I hear, I see,
I know.

AFTER THE FOURTH

Fireworks are over.
    I'm headed home. The after-smoke
dances with Patsy Cline's "Crazy"
    as a stray rocket rises
above macadam and black pines.
    It's been eleven years.

Next day's noon snooze
    then wake, it's still summer.
Same month, same week,
    same day on the porch,
the ash trimmed gold
    and a slow hazy breeze.

Nightfall, counting down
    fourteen days, Sparky, Rufus, and I.
A random boom startles us
    snuggled-up on the couch,
a Fourth of July afterthought
    rattling our tea and ice cream.

Overall we're okay, dogs and me, yet
    I miss the strange way he phrases things,
his odd logic, how a graying beard
    sends my neck a-chill
when the mercury's
    ninety-nine degrees.

THE STATION

The Algonquin, his phone call.
Dark novel, Redgrave's
eyes center stage.

Home again. A knocking
at the screen door,
Parkinson's. Let it in?

Scenes creep up, forgotten
lines, curtain calls, waiting
to hear from *The Times*.

There is a deadening.
Wooden arms
fall and clang

incoming train.

PRESSING IN

Reddened
by day's sun

toes press
in cooling sand.

The moon
quivers

on shifting waves.
Our hands link

unlink, two
pale butterflies.

A tunnel, Time
at the end

the end of breath,
hanging

and waterlogged,
a heavy moon.

Half-laughing,
you turn me

my shoulders
from the moon

to warmth
pressing in

here,
in your deep eyes

an eternity of stars.

one flesh

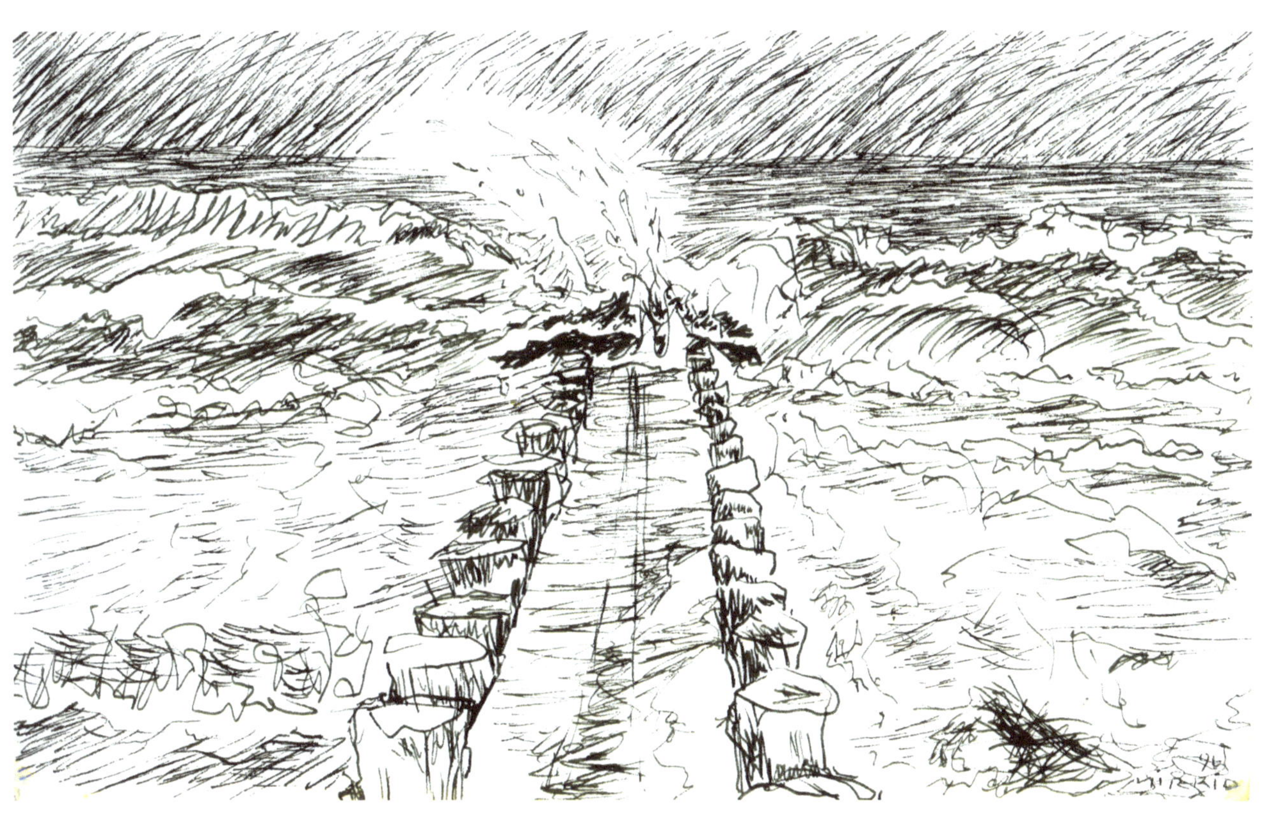

CLASSROOM G

These old standards
take me back,
nights I took my turns

on Daddy's shoes, me
a real live dolly
with a dark patch on her gown.

Me and Daddy,
Fred and Ginger
and the Big Band sounds.

Now you and I hear Morely,
smaller steps, right and right
and left and left, and ball change.

We bump and drag
on cracked linoleum
in pea green classroom G.

Then the girl from Ipanema
enters, takes your hand
and *ahhh…*

utters secrets
in your silver beard, whispers
love me, never leave me

as your agile body
guides her
through a room of sparkling stardust

with a slowly rising,
hypnotizing
Fred and Ginger moon.

CELL MEMORY

like a gull
upon water

you warm
my secret

place
your lips

fingertips
listen

to a song
long forgotten

my hot
joy

springs
from so long ago

only cells
remember

how it had grown so cold

CLEARING

Held at the tip
of a narrow aqua rod,
the white pill enters
into my body,
into a channel
thinning, shrinking,
skin so reluctant to stretch
I heard myself mumble
No more.

Soon, very soon
a second breath,
eagerly filling
the lung's crevices,
sucking in
the heady scent.
A joyful rolling
in fresh clover,
and we bow

to the sun
at day's end,
its burning embers.
We know our bodies
in this clearing
will fail again,
and our hands
open in prayer.

child-poet

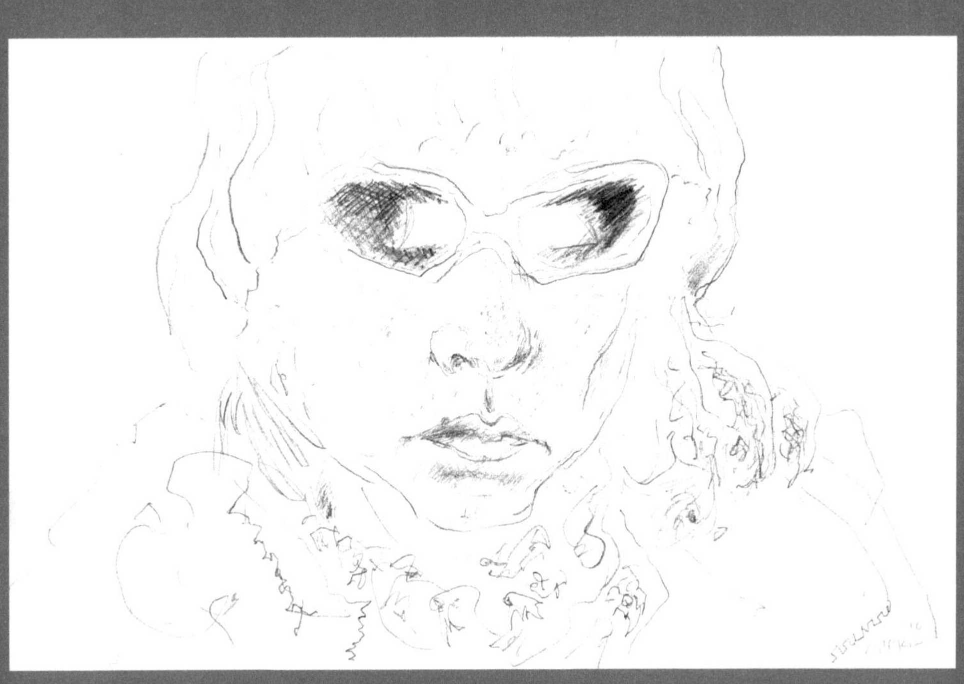

ODE TO MONA

How I adore
the Mona Lisa smile,
the mystery

the mastery, the
Did she now, or didn't she?
pregnant pause

savoir faire,
her guile.
Is bitter sweet?

Is life complete
without her,
art would skip a beat

yes Mona, Mona, Mona
is the toast!
Oh how I crave

the Mona Lisa smile,
and yet I'll need
to learn of self-control.

Ne'er kiss and tell,
nor rush pell-mell.
I'll need to work

at gentle perk,
to cool the cauldron
of my boiling soul.

WETPRINT

sometimes the best part
of a half-mile swim
at the gym
is what happens after.

water pounds hot
on scalp, shoulders,
soap bubbles race
down arms, belly.

towel dry, then
enter the stall
and feel freedom
releasing hot pee.

then there's something
flat and wet
below the cubicle door.
An unusual map

its far end rounded,
and nearest,
a line of five dots
one big, four small

then a curve
with an odd bump,
not built for delicate shoes!
I can't turn away...

warmth
for a lost child
still shivering.
Yet the toe dots

imperfect curve
and rounded heel fade,
until only dry tiles

tell of this visitation.

LITTLE JIB

Barely heard,
a face in the corner.
Snapshot,
a shattered family.

So you raise your lavender jib,
sail the Lake of Four Winds,
sow teardrops into clouds
in a turquoise sky.

You come to a land of
wildflowers, honeysuckle
and gentle horses
welcoming you.

Deep in the woods
there's a snake-shaped log
and light, a giant rock
for weaving words.

The rock your Jesus hears you.
Your bright and morning star
calls, *Return and learn*
how big you really are.

BRUSHING OUT

If I outlive dogs,
husband, and heaven forbid
children, not to mention
grandchildren, and if
I need wheeling from
commode to motorized bed,
if hands shake

so no one can read
my handwriting, my voice
too thin to speak into a machine,
I might still, unless
eyesight's clouded or brain muddled,
be able to grasp
pencil, pen, or brush

like the seasoned Matisse,
arm with pole to ceiling
brushing out weeping trees,
water-laden clouds,
and nine black stars
around a withering moon,
enough to make a young dog howl.

least of these

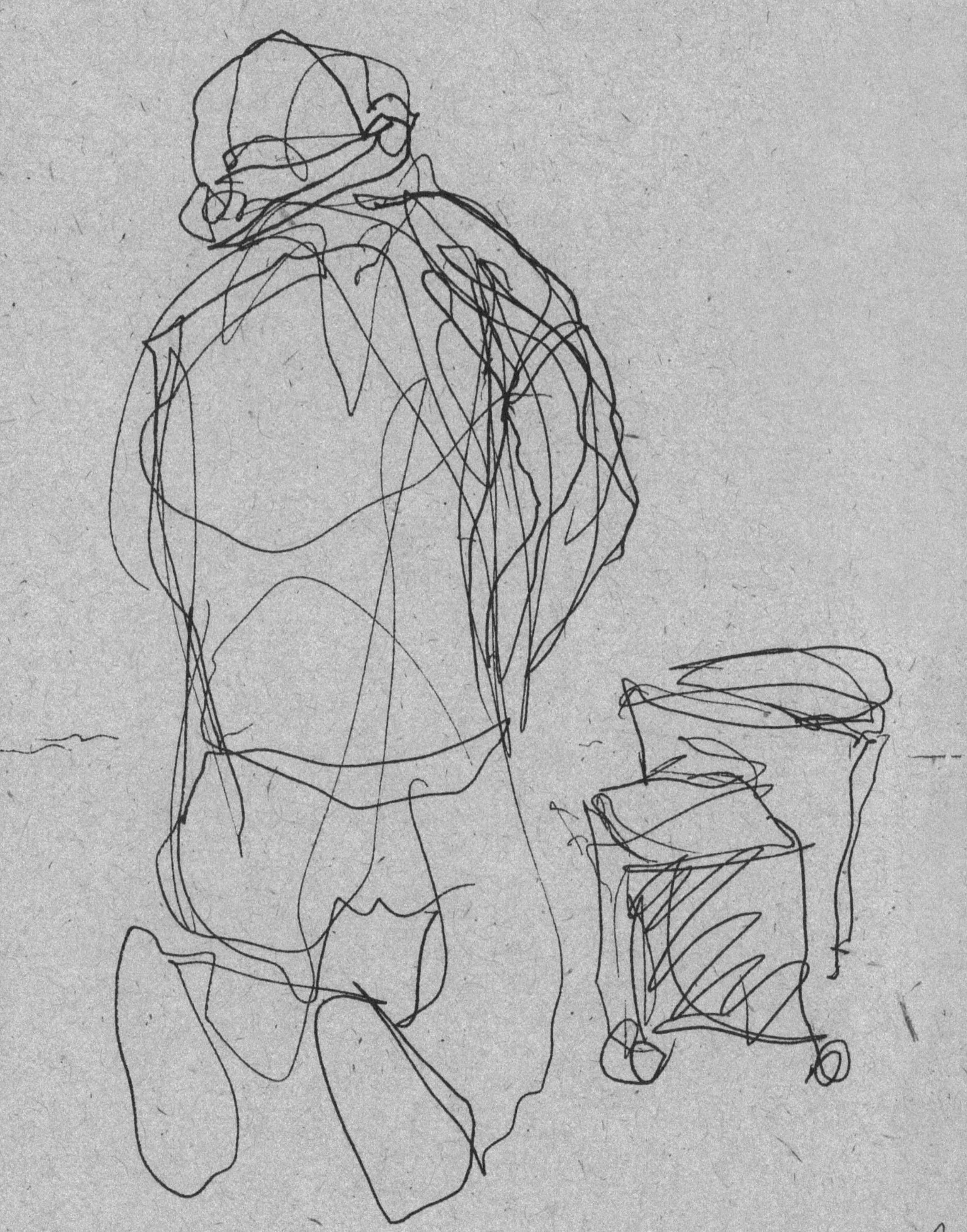

RED GLOVES

There, through the well lit window
the upscale dinner crowd.
We step up out of the snow
and breath clouds disappear.

Wishing merely to sample,
he and I take a cafe table
past the quarter-mile case of
French pastries and chocolate mousse.

Starting to feel the warmth
we clink our eight dollar goblets
to our connectedness.
Then through the door

in her threadbare coat,
wild-eyed, hat slumped over one ear,
scuffs up to the bread man
and in a raspy voice, *Do you have*

a bag, not too big.
Though she already holds one
or two, even three
and she waits, looking to the right

then to the left, fidgets a bit,
stuffs the crisp Sarabeth's bag
into her pile, shuffles out the door,
short white breaths, shoes in snow.

Woman in a Donald Brooks dress
excuses herself,
inquires through the doorway
Do you have any gloves?

Seeing raw hands
she returns to her chair, purse,
then out the door
to begin coaxing

red leather gloves
over ten gnarled fingers,
each attempting to receive
the scent of belonging.

BAIT 'N' SWITCH

O precious hermit crab,

your home's a simple shell —
it keeps you safe,
a flowing cloak,
a welcomed bed.

Yet a flamboyant artist

bought you and ten others,
added sand and plants —
installed a large aquarium
inside a New York gallery.

And little did you know

he had created
shells of glass —
aqua, peach, pale green,
no less than seventeen

and guessing when you grew

you'd leave your shell
its crust, its barnacles
and crawl into the new —
your private inner self

a spectacle for all to view!

O precious one
what will you do, who will you be
the times you crave the dark,
beloved room to hear

and breathe,
and see.

PAPER SHREDDER

Under a sooty chin,
fingers pick
a wad of paper towel.

Hair knotted,
head cocked to one side
speaks to the mirror.

It's pride, isn't it?
echoes off
bathroom walls.

Pride makes it
so you don't ask
for anything!

Leaning over sinks,
Would you like
a sip of my beer?

Stench of her body
sickens.
I run.

She trails me
on the concourse,
past ticket windows

and yells,
You know, a man once
took a sip

then he went and bought me
a sandwich! and she weaves
through rush hour briefcases

and three piece suits.
Not like ones
trying their luck

against the wall,
God bless you,
I'm hungry.

I race to lower levels.
Trains come in,
miles… a mirror

strange bathroom,
a ten year old crying.
Apartment, boxes, no dog

no rope swing,
no Dad. Cars scream
like cats in heat.

Nights on her back.
No appetite, morning
picking her warts

then school,
two crosstown blocks,
wait for bus, *pull cord to stop*.

Through blue doors,
sea of blue and white tunics.
Remember to breathe. Strange teachers.

Girls with secrets.
Bathroom. Eyes dart.
Bell for lunch. A tray, a seat

alone. Red jello
and mashed potatoes.
The bell.

If only they wouldn't
see it,
this thing in my lap!

On the tray a rat's nest,
size of her fist.
White shredded paper.

little ones

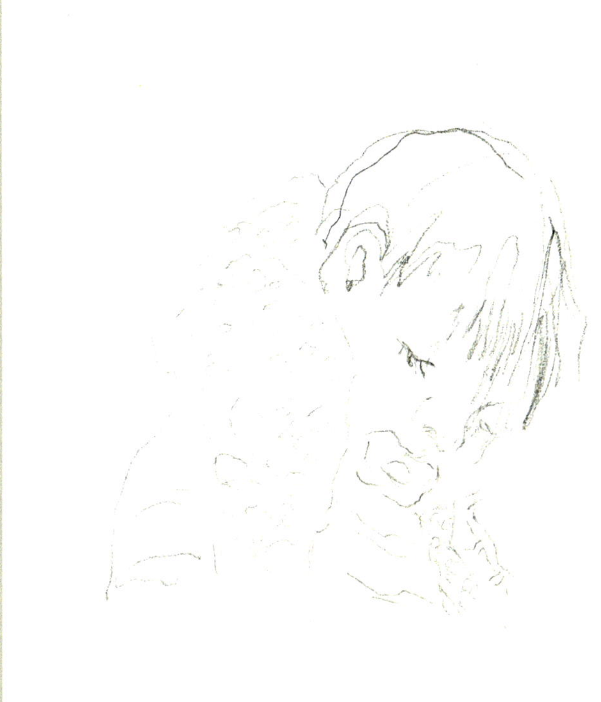

KENT TEKULVE'S SHOELACES
(for Eddy and Drew)

Decades old cassette
plays like
a worn-out washing machine.

Yet boy voices
emerge from the fog. I lean closer,
my older son, only six

Kent Tekulve,
he's really good, he pitches sidearm
for the Pirates!

Loud static.
Then more words,
my younger son asking

How'd I tie my shoes, Mommy?
Again the static. And I hunger
at the edge

for crumbs
from an aging ribbon.

DEAR RUFUS

King Ru, so refined,
your tail, your nose,
how well you dance the arabesque
around your gilded throne!

Each new day pleases
as you survey the outer reaches
of your realm (clearly at the helm!)
Rufus the King.

Thus humbly we wait
here at the gate.
Hoping beyond hope to hear
the lowly hinge declare

"Your Highness's
presence at the door!"

So dutifully we bow
and stroke the very velvet
of your ears, embrace
the royal fur.

Always quick to utter
the prescribed words,
taking care our eyes
are never meeting yours.

Please Your Majesty, please
just a word, Sir Rufus, King.
There does remain one curiosity
concerning our indentured servitude.

It's something so profound
yet simple (beg your pardon!)
you can't see.
There really isn't any *need*

for your servants to be shackled.
For if we weren't
such loyal lackeys of the royal crown,
we'd love you *anyway*.

If only you'd step down!

MOONBEAMS
(for Ty)

A little patch
of moonlight sits
on the floor.

Not a scrap
of paper I'd missed
from before.

Brushed it
with my toe, only
air, nothing more.

In the yard,
ash trees like hands
held high.

What will they catch
in the deep
night sky?

Just crickets
fiddlin' on wet
leaves of June.

Child, I can't
come to see you
before August's full moon.

But now
somethings's rippling
the curtain seams!

There's a song
riding in on midnight's
moonbeams.

I can hear,
almost see you,
little one, sing!

lost, found

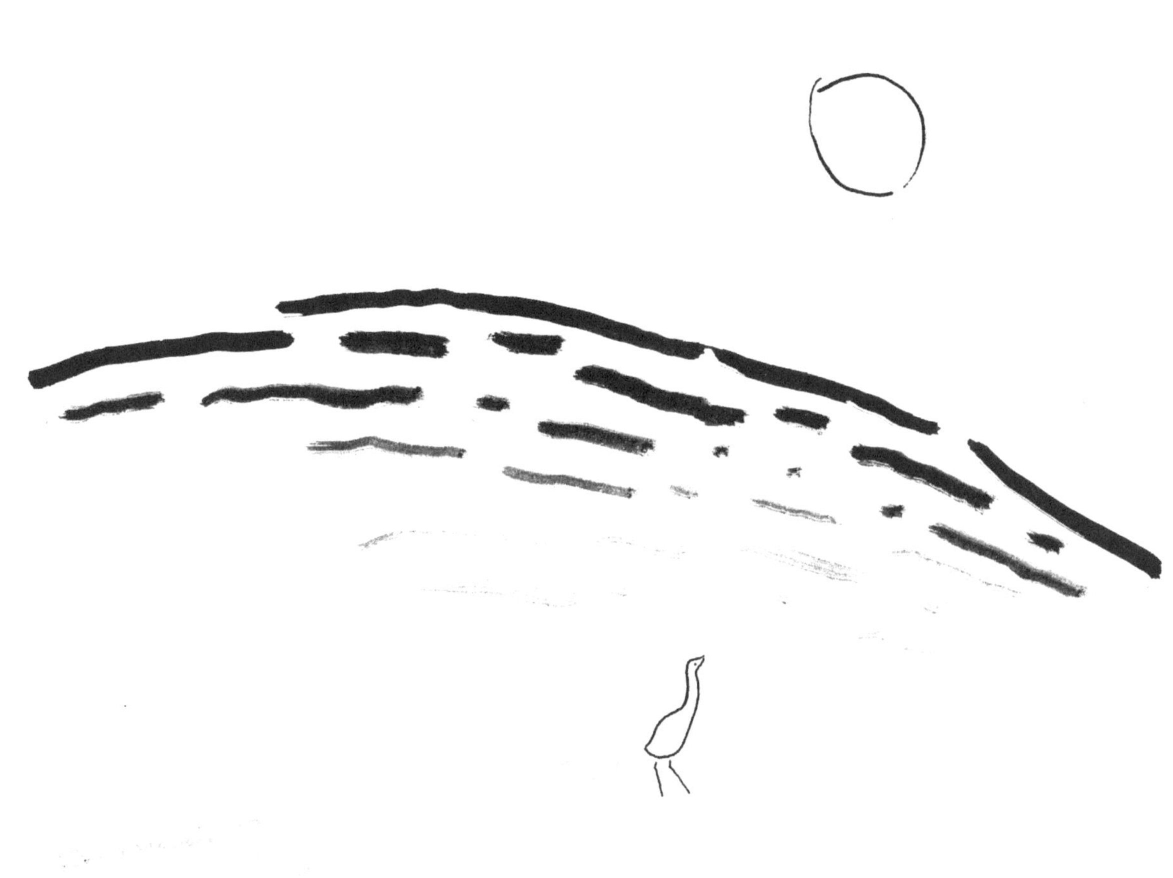

EYE AM

she was there and yet she wasn't,
but she was beautiful and she was chic.
she was kind and then she wasn't,
but man could she play "mountain greenery"!

she's gone and yet she isn't,
still living in my dreams and fears.
i've tried and failed to win her heart
for all these thirty years.

today my purse was stolen.
now i'm in my studio,
eyes wet, red and swollen.
when i open them

in front of me, on my painting
of her cool, dismissive face
there's a Divine eye! alive and loving me.
it's her eye too, not the mom i knew

but the one You created her to be,
loving You *and seeing me, the real me*.
i feel like ten again!
yet mended in Your light

now i'm her precious one.
dear Lord i am forever in Your debt
and *thank you, thank you,* i'm so happy
i am hers and she's forever, ever mine!

STUFF OF LIFE

Is it
the way one
grips the brush,
pressure
on tapered sable
through a drift
of thick rose madder.

Or is it
gray matter
suddenly lighter,
its essence
exiting the body
unnoticed,
a grace note before.

HARBOR

In their room of twilight blue,
late afternoon shadows.
Nearby, baby Andrew sleeps.

I have not been like this,
in my son's house, in such peace.
There, above the ivory couch

is my father's painting,
the Italian harbor. It's calm here,
in this reverie

until a ray of light enters
the left edge of the canvas
and with seeing fingers

travels,
one vertical strip
at a time, awakening

luscious creams.
A sky of icing blue,
creamsicle roofs

waves of mint and plum,
and lemon-butter sails
trimmed under vanilla clouds.

The waves dance,
sails billow, and the sky
is ripe with music.

For in this light lives
my father's hearty laugh, his warmth
and his well-crafted tales.

Yet as the beam
nears the harbor's final edge,
it begins to weaken

fade,
then falls
into shadows of dusk.

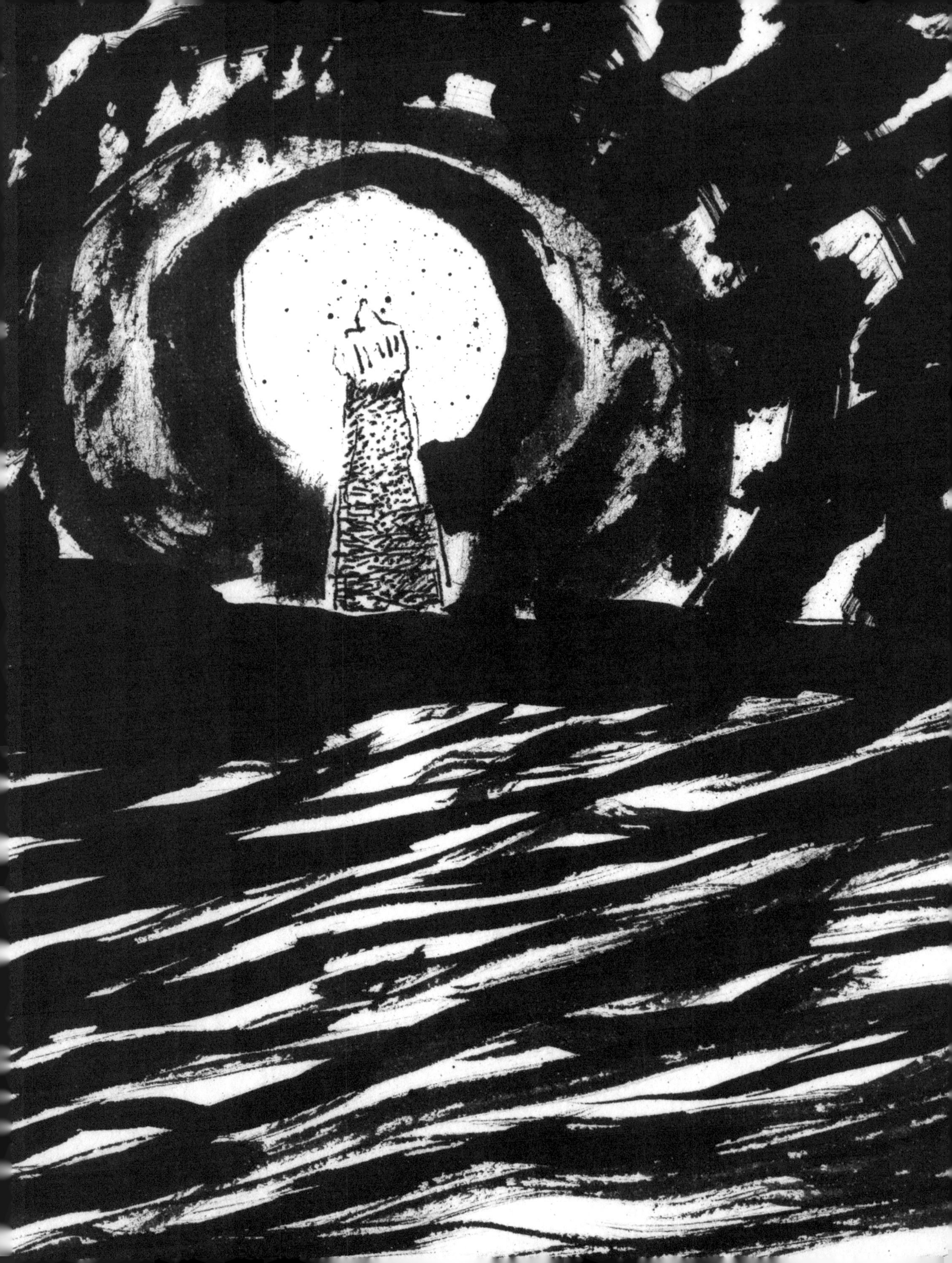

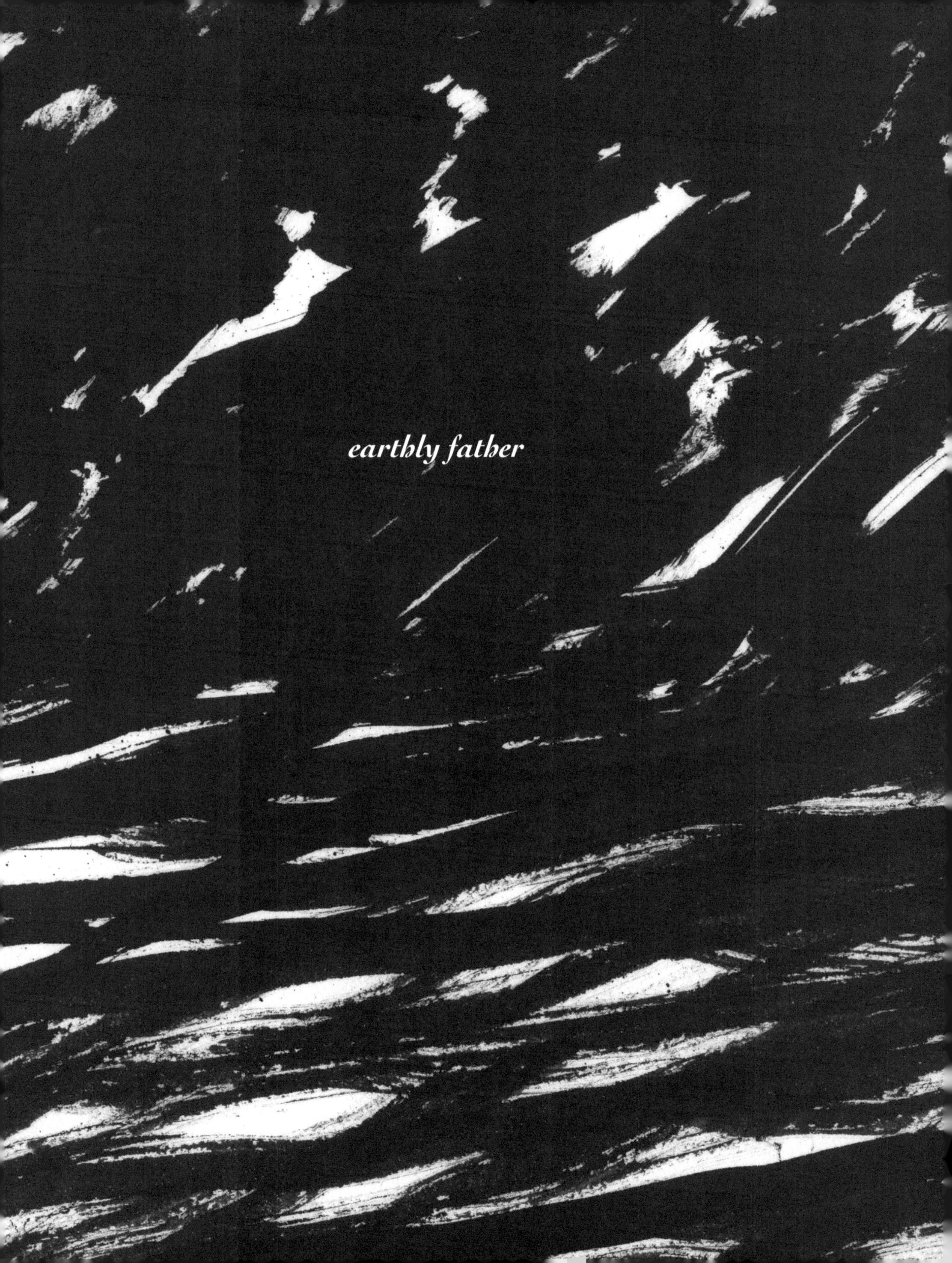

earthly father

FADING

The back of your hands
Are stained blue-black,
Lungs frail, fed
By a thin clear tube.

Who will be
Like you, insisting I call
From home, even before
My key turns in the lock.

Who will be
Stronger than mid-day sun
When I enter the room.
When you're gone

Who will rescue me,
Be near, who will
Dampen the ticking
Of my watch.

PLAID BLANKET

He's breathing steadily now.
No lit signals
spiking up and down,
nurses in and out
air too close.

In the elevator
mirrored walls, doors open
to a darkened snack café
chair legs up,
food cases vacant.

Floors glaring,
daring me to find a way out.
Catch an extra breath, extra
step, and there's
no one.

The night
an angry hawk,
daggered claws and beak
ready to tear.
I bolt to the car.

In, slam the door,
lean on padded wheel
with its low steady idle,
shaky knees calmed
under the plaid blanket

the one he kept in back
where baby sister and I
warmed ourselves,
listening as his words became light
in the sharp winter air.

amazing grace

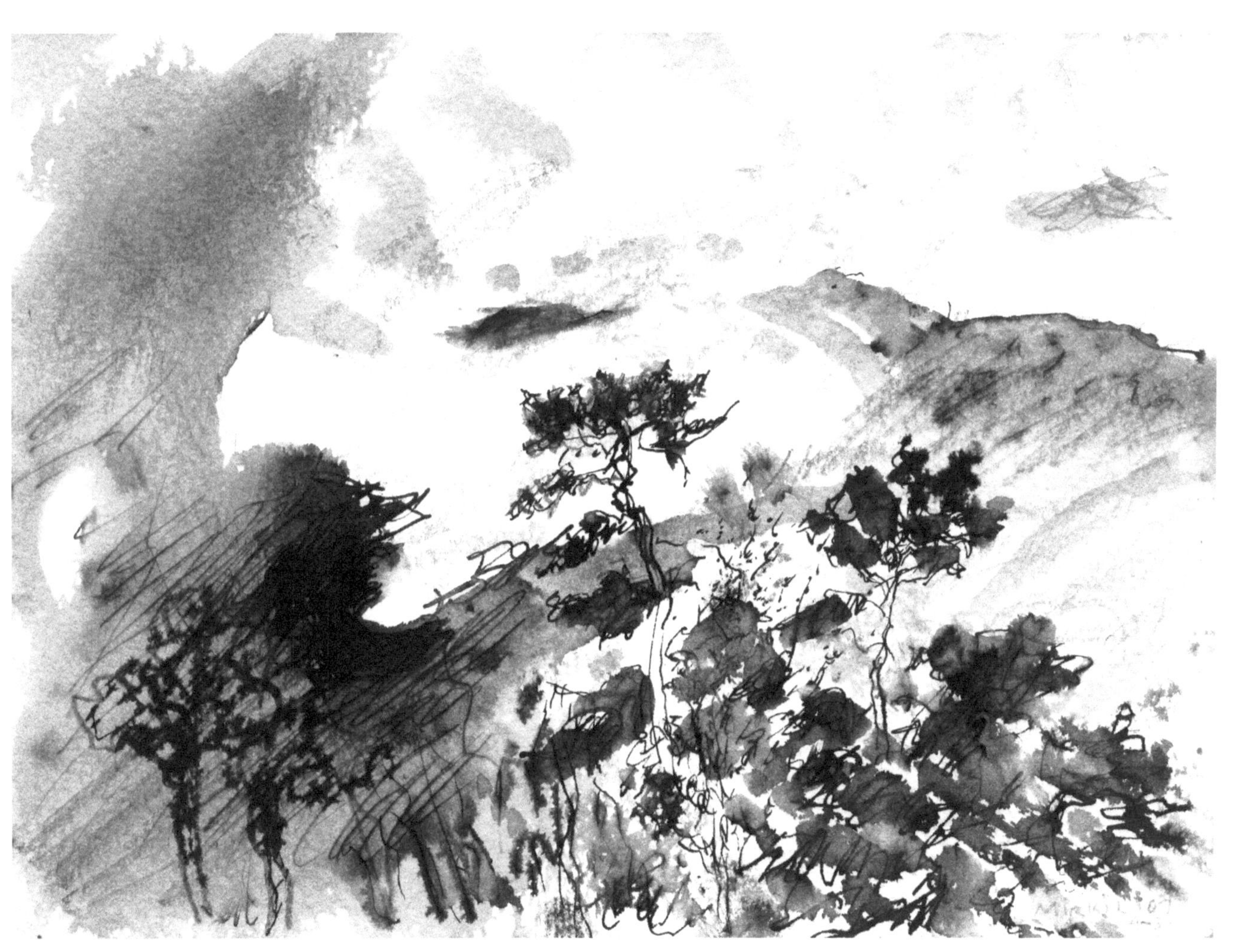

IN YOUR LIGHT
(Psalm 23, a midrash)

My Lord leads me
through a valley
of clover and trillium.
We wade in living waters
and my heart grows wings!

One night alone
in my tent, terrors penetrate
the darkness.
Help me,
Jesus help me!

My Savior hears.
In His light
I paint my rage, like lava
from my wounds.
I paint my joy.

Father in Heaven,
Holy Spirit of Jesus,
Healer of my soul,
Hallelujah! I am made new!
Lord, You are my life!

DEEP TO DEEP

They call You
Prince of Peace, Rabboni,
also Lamb, but on the strand
You whispered *Ocean,*
yes, I AM.

I am afraid
of depths, of thundering waves.
The undertow sucks me out
near people without teeth
in rotting homes and unmarked graves.

You say, *Don't be afraid,*
the waves, the shallow hands
upon the sand are mine.
They skim and bubble,
lay a mirror for the sky.

Yes there is deep, my child.
My dark is womb. Your wound is safe.
And I will give you depths more beautiful
than you have ever known,
my seedling in the sun.

Ocean, I'm lonely and afraid.
Are you lonely too?
I'll stretch my arms out,
close my eyes
and dive.

O Lord, You are
the glistening sea, The Light!
I dance!
Inside Your love,
Your life inside of me.

I want to be!

GRAVITY FLIGHT

Over the edge, Sir Isaac!
The apple core's in flight.
We watch it arc, above cacti
raising arms to blinding light.
Nothing's purely science.

This missile seems suspended
over tilting desert floor,
a natural Elizabethan stage.
Offstage, director's voice is calm
and sure and not too far away.

It's as if all creation listens.
Warty toad, thorny plants
layers in the rock,
the shocking white of clouds.
How unlike modern life!

The soul's becoming one with dreams,
a valley of ecstatic flight.
The ledge, the deepening breath, the leap!
Gliding within inches
of a bloody tango with the land.

Is this love's flight, the dance?
What of love's weight?
Chance a being won't survive
without Divine romance.

ACKNOWLEDGMENTS

My earliest thanks to Miss Ross, who in eighth grade offered an elective poetry class in a tiny mezzanine room at the Nightingale Bamford School. Under her valuable instruction I first expressed myself through poetry and was introduced to the critique process.

My husband Brian is poetry critic-in-residence. Without his urging, *Sower* would not have been produced at this time. Brian is open to giving his insights often within a day or two of my first draft, which is a real blessing to me. Jean Brown has been reading my poetry for over a decade, placing my work in a context in which I would only dare to dream. Gene Rochberg has been a fountain of support and enthusiasm. I am touched by how she values poems I give her as meal tickets and as birthday gifts. Bill Hollis has given me wonderfully wise suggestions. Grazie, Bill. Carolyn Markle has taken a special interest in my working on this book, and has been generous with ideas of how to get it out into the world. And in my letters to Andrew Mangravite over the years, I have enclosed many poems. I am grateful for Andy's honest responses and ongoing encouraging words. For years Joanne Leva has been generating the growth of a poetry community in Montgomery County, Pennsylvania. Because of her programs I began reading my poems in public. Thank you, Joanne!

To sharpen my skills over the years I have sought out many sources for critiques. About four years ago I spent a year working on this text with Daniel Spinella, a patient and skillful poetry editor. This began *Sower's* official journey. Dan, thank you for the tools you gave me to become a better writer.

Most recently I was invited to join Wordshop, a critique group of twelve poets including several Montgomery and Bucks County Poet Laureates. For me it's like being called up from the farm team. Many thanks to the members of Wordshop for your poems, your critiques, and your friendship. Working with the group has been invaluable — akin to a graduate level program in poetry. Over the past year with newly learned skills I have reworked the entire manuscript, and when finished I'd revised every poem.

I am indebted to my readers: Cynthia Chase, Andrew Mangravite, Patsy Stroud, and Michael Rose, for their thoughtful responses to this manuscript. I would also like to thank Veronica Miller, the book designer. Veronica, thank you for your patience during my extensive revisions. And thank you especially for your design—it's a work of art!

Amy Small-McKinney has been a blessing, giving me suggestions from her years of writing, refining, and getting poems published. While Amy was working on her recent book I met her publishers, Jon Pastor and Meg Kennedy of BookArts Press. The rest is history. Not only are Jon and Meg a joy to work with but they are wonderful people. I would also like to thank my proofreaders, Laura Bauder and Dick Lee for their time and willingness to help with a tedious task in the finishing process.

A toast to poets and lyricists past and present who inspire and give me courage. I am grateful to Leonard Gontarek whose wisdom and poetry continue to help bring my poems closer to the essential. Mary Karr's *Sinners Welcome* has allowed me to feel less alone in expressing my faith through poetry. I must also thank Emily Dickinson, George Herbert, John Donne, the Book of Isaiah, the Psalms, Hymns, Anna Akhmatova, Rumi, Kay Ryan, Rainer Maria Rilke, Virginia Hamilton Adair, Jean Valentine, R.S. Thomas, May Sarton, Stephen Sondheim, Sheryl Noethe, W.S. Merwin, Adrianne Rich, Claudia Emerson, Kenneth Patchen, Louise Glück, and Sharon Olds. They touch the place in my soul where poetry is born.

And since the first shall be last, I am prayerful in thanking the still small voice, the Holy Spirit of Jesus, Lord over all creation, King of all Kings, Lord of all Lords, Heavenly Father, Prince of Peace, Jesus my deliverer, the Word made flesh.

ABOUT THE AUTHOR

Helen Mirkil's poems have appeared in such publications as *Apiary, Art Times, The Bucks County Writer*, and *Ruah.* She participates in poetry readings in the Philadelphia region. Also an accomplished visual artist, Helen earned both undergraduate and graduate degrees at the Pennsylvania Academy of the Fine Arts, and has exhibited at galleries in the U.K. as well as numerous venues on the east coast including solo exhibitions at the Berman Museum of Art, University of Mary Washington, and in New York City.

Helen's life is filled with the gifts of marriage, family, and friends, as well as her passion for dance, art, music, and poetry. She accumulates US Airways frequent flyer miles going to North Carolina to visit sons Eddy and Drew, daughters-in-law Adrianne and Nnenne, as well as three adorable grandsons Ty, Oliver, and Andrew. They, along with Helen's dear Sparky (and until recently dear Rufus, bless him!) make her empty nest full again.

"My greatest challenge in life," Helen says, "is to receive the mystery of the Holy Spirit of Jesus living inside me… focusing on His character, humbled by His sacrifice on the Cross — learning to see my hands and feet as His hands and feet — and to drink of the Heavenly Father's perfect love and forgiveness."

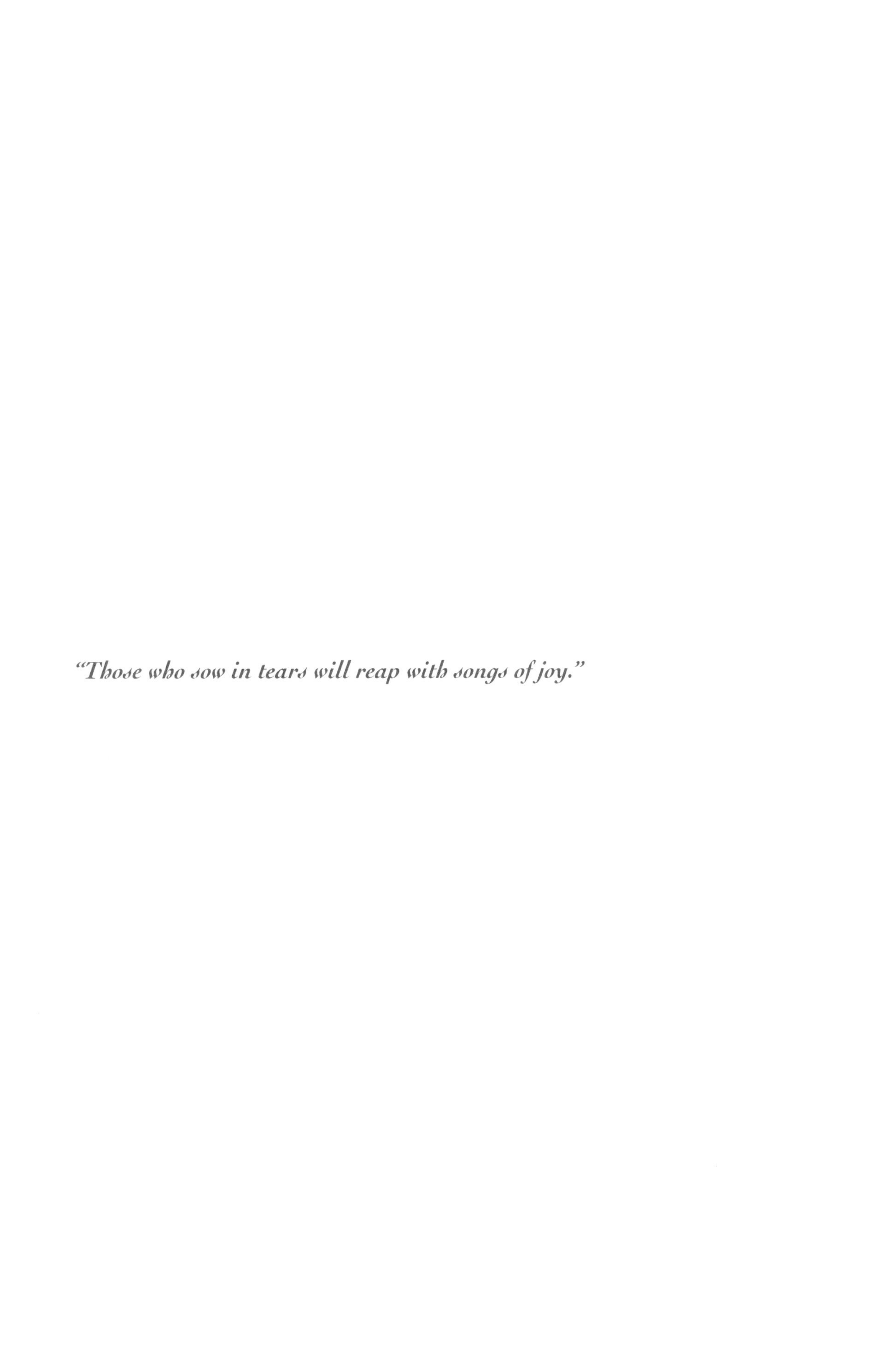

"Those who sow in tears will reap with songs of joy."

www.ingramcontent.com/pod-product-compliance
Lightning Source LLC
LaVergne TN
LVHW070138110826
845147LV00002B/283

* 9 7 8 0 9 7 9 5 8 6 1 5 6 *